P9-DDI-817

SandCastle
Let's Go!

LET'S GO

BY

CABLE CAR

ANDERS HANSON

Consulting Editor, Diane Craig, M.A./Reading Specialist

ABDO Publishing Company

Published by ABDO Publishing Company, 8000 West 78th Street, Edina, MN 55439.

Printed in the United States.

Editor: Pam Price
Curriculum Coordinator: Nancy Tuminelly
Cover and Interior Design and Production: Mighty Media
Photo Credits: Linda Goldman, Shutterstock; cable car illustration, Louis R. Biro
Special thanks to Barbara Corsbie, Val Lupiz, Joe Thompson (www.cable-car-guy.com), and the San Francisco Municipal Railway. "San Francisco Municipal Railway" is a registered service mark of the city and county of San Francisco.

Library of Congress Cataloging-in-Publication Data

Hanson, Anders, 1980-
   Let's go by cable car / Anders Hanson.
     p. cm. -- (Let's go!)
   ISBN 978-1-59928-896-3
   1. Street-railroads--Juvenile literature. 2. Cable cars (Streetcars)--Juvenile literature. 3. Railroads, Cable--Juvenile literature. 4. San Francisco--Juvenile literature. I. Title. II. Title: Cable car. III. Series.

TF148.H3245 2008
388.4'6--dc22

2007013408

SandCastle™ Level: Transitional

SandCastle™ books are created by a team of professional educators, reading specialists, and content developers around five essential components—phonemic awareness, phonics, vocabulary, text comprehension, and fluency—to assist young readers as they develop reading skills and increase their general knowledge. All books are written, reviewed, and leveled for guided reading, early intervention reading, and Accelerated Reader® programs for use in shared, guided, and independent reading and writing activities to support a balanced approach to literacy instruction. The SandCastle™ series has four levels that correspond to early literacy development. The levels are provided to help teachers and parents select appropriate books for young readers.

Emerging Readers
(no flags)

Beginning Readers
(1 flag)

Transitional Readers
(2 flags)

Fluent Readers
(3 flags)

SandCastle™ would like to hear from you. Please send us your comments or questions.

sandcastle@abdopublishing.com

A cable car moves
by gripping and
releasing a moving
cable that runs
under the street.

3

Cable cars
run on tracks.

A turntable turns the cable car around.

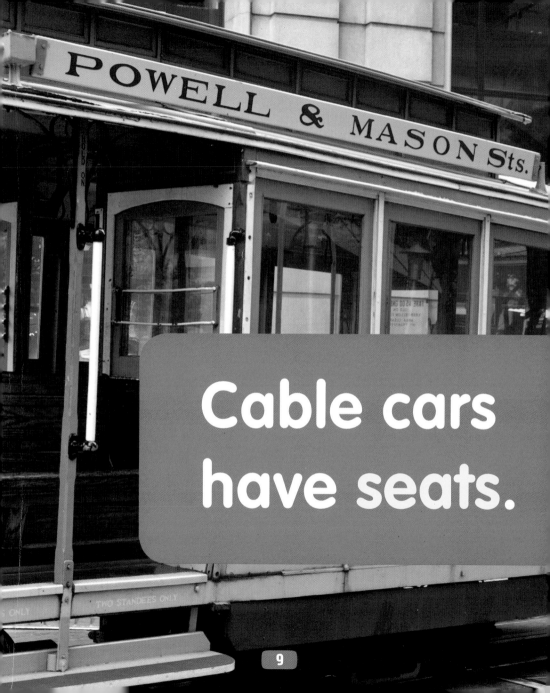

Cable cars
have seats.

A cable car
has a bell
on its roof.

One ring of the bell signals to stop. Two rings means go.

HOLD ON

HOLD ON

MASON

DANGER
DO NOT LEAN OUT

13

The gripman starts and stops the cable car. Gloves protect the gripman's hands.

Barb gives the conductor her ticket. She likes to ride on cable cars.

San Francisco
has cable cars.
The cable cars go
up and down the
steep hills.

HAVE YOU BEEN
ON A CABLE CAR?

WHERE DID YOU GO?

CABLE CAR PARTS

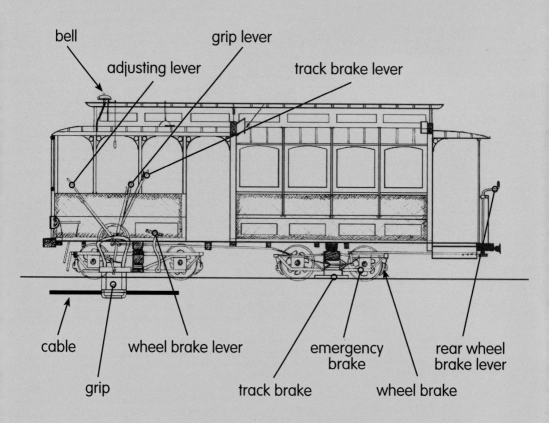

bell

adjusting lever

grip lever

track brake lever

cable

wheel brake lever

grip

track brake

emergency
brake

wheel brake

rear wheel
brake lever

Cable cars were invented in San Francisco in 1873.

Each year, the San Francisco Municipal Railway holds a cable car bell-ringing contest.

The cable that the cable cars grip runs at a steady nine and a half miles per hour.

GLOSSARY

cable – a strong, thick rope made up of many wires or fibers.

conductor – the person whose job is to be in charge of a bus, train, or street car.

grip – in a cable car, the device that holds and releases the cable.

signal – to send a message using a sound, sign, or device agreed to in advance.

steep – having a very sharp slope.

To see a complete list of SandCastle™ books and other nonfiction titles from ABDO Publishing Company, visit **www.abdopublishing.com**.

8000 West 78th Street, Edina, MN 55439 • 800-800-1312 • 952-831-1632 fax